THE MONACELLI PRESS

# TEXAS
THE HOUSE
# MADE
AND
# TEXAS
THE LAND
# MODERN

HELEN THOMPSON
Photographs by Casey Dunn
Foreword by Lawrence W. Speck

# CONTENTS

# FOREWORD

## Lawrence W. Speck

There is a popular myth that great architects achieve prominence by developing their own personal "style" and that a great building is some sort of art object that sits in abstract space (or in a photograph) as an iconic monument to its author's ego and personal predilections. A far more attractive and significant definition of a great building, however, acknowledges the power of place and culture as the seminal generator of design and reveres the role of the architect as the perceptive interpreter of those critical forces—someone who brings them poetically into tangible physical form.

Frank Lloyd Wright is one of those accused of ego-driven self-expression, but there is a much deeper and nuanced understanding of his work that sees him accurately as a consummate interpreter of place and culture. At the same time in his mature career that he was designing Fallingwater, which is an extraordinary embodiment of its lush, terraced site in hilly Western Pennsylvania, he was also working on Taliesin West, which beautifully expresses the stark flatness of the powerful desert terrain in Arizona. Landscape, climate, materials, and cultural heritage of the places Wright worked were an essential inspiration for the best of his work, as they have been for great designers throughout the history of architecture.

The architects whose work is represented in this book are not focused on their own signature style or on fashionable forms and motifs that are "hot" for the moment in trendy architectural publications. Instead they seek seminal ideas and character for their work in the realities of the particular situations where they find themselves building, and Texas—the place where their work is focused—offers an abundance of powerful realities.

Long lauded for its big sky, its endless horizons, its minimalist starkness, and its mythic scale, Texas is much more than that. Its variety of landscape character, both at the micro level of a few square miles and at the macro level of the whole state, is both enriching and confusing. A mere five-mile crossing of the Palo Duro Canyon in the Texas Panhandle bridges radical changes in temperature, vegetation, wildlife, and topography as well as colors, materials, textures, and light qualities. A trip across the state vertically from Brownsville to

Alpine to Abilene and Amarillo offers everything from flat tropical farmlands to rugged mountain peaks to desert wastelands to vast savannas and grasslands.

There is no singular Texas regional style because there is no singular Texas climate, landscape, or character. But there is a stalwart cadre of architects who have, for decades, worked as a loosely bound, multi-generational group to create, collectively, a sincere interpretation of this powerful place with its many nuanced variations. Their work, beautifully collected in this book, does achieve a kind of cohesiveness when viewed together. Like the individual architects themselves, the houses share values and approach and an overt desire to create an appropriate and memorable place.

Though this work is clearly expressive of its time, it is more visceral, tactile, and personally engaging than most houses that are called "modernist." In terms of links to pioneering modern work in the first half of the twentieth century, the houses in this book are more akin to the ethos created by Alvar Aalto for the buildings he designed in Finland or to those by Frank Lloyd Wright for the American Midwest than they are to the works of modern masters like Mies van der Rohe or Le Corbusier. There is a strong connection to people and culture in these buildings—a "humanism," to use Aalto's term—that is absent in the those of the International Style.

Houses rooted in eternal verities of landscape, climate, and culture grow better with age. They take root and settle in. They welcome the life and inhabitation of their owners, even over multiple generations. It is refreshing to see the older dowagers in this book taking new life and to see the more recent ones gaining experience and patina.

It is very satisfying to see these disparate but related projects gathered together by Helen Thompson. The houses are truly beautiful in Casey Dunn's elegant photographs, but they are even more moving when they are experienced in person. The phenomenological presence of this kind of architecture far exceeds any virtual experience. They are delightful places to view in a book, amazing places to visit, and truly extraordinary places for living.

# INTRODUCTION

When you see a modern house, you know it. Brash, lots of glass, radiating the shock of the new even though it's been a century since the movement began, the architectural juggernaut powered through a world impatient to shake off the cultural excesses of the nineteenth century. The new aesthetic rejected the grandiosity of Victorian, Beaux-Arts, and neoclassical architecture, a repudiation that signaled a wondrous leap in the direction of the bold and the new. Modernism exuded authority, and it had an unequivocal look. Le Corbusier, the Swiss-French architect, designer, painter, urban planner, and writer, enumerated five characteristics:

- Load-bearing columns to replace supporting walls
- Open floor plans
- Facades unencumbered by structural constraints
- Horizontal windows that light rooms equally
- Roof gardens

Modernism was a perfect fit in Texas, where prosperity boomed and new technology begat structural and manufacturing advancements. But, the use of broad expanses of glass, so alluring as a hallmark of the style, was also its most glaring weakness—in Texas, at least. This was clear to two iconoclastic Dallas architects who fervently believed that modernist design in their state should take into account local nuances that the international movement ignored.

David Williams and O'Neil Ford co-opted the modernist movement with their own version of what modern should look like in a state where topography, climate, and culture are powerful. The land and the climate were so compelling, in fact, that it made no sense to these two contrarians to create buildings that did not acknowledge their influence. David Williams expressed his ideas in a fall 1928 article in the *Southwest Review,* illustrated by O'Neil Ford with his drawings of buildings in Castroville, San Antonio, Salado, and Moody:

> In the many beautiful little houses left scattered over Texas by early settlers, there is full proof that some of our grandfathers and most of our great-grandfathers possessed the refined taste and culture for which we have been searching abroad . . . so that they began building, not as they had built in England or France or Germany, but to suit their own needs and to satisfy as best they could the exactions of climate and the limitations of the natural materials to be found close at hand. The houses they made . . . seemed to grow out of the ground on which they stood; and they were beautiful because they were simple and natural.

If ever there was an architectural movement that sprang from the joy of discovery, Texas regionalism—as it came to be called—is it. Discovery was rampant during the early 1930s in Texas, a period of extraordinary freshness and vitality in the intellectual life of the state. Williams and Ford were right in the middle of it all, if not actually fanning the flames. Williams was gregarious and well connected in Dallas literary, art, and historical circles, and he introduced Ford to what was considered the Dallas Left Bank. These influencers were fascinated by the idea that they could develop a regional culture in the Southwest. They included the artist, art critic, and later museum director Jerry Bywaters. Also a professor at Southern Methodist University, Bywaters was a leader in the group of artists known as the Dallas Nine, a coterie of painters, printmakers, and sculptors, whose art was inspired by the land and people of the Southwest. Lon Tinkle, a French professor at SMU was soon a friend; Tinkle was also the book editor for the *Dallas Morning News* and Ford's neighbor in "Culture Gulch." Williams and Ford began contributing to the *Southwest Review*, along with other notables such as historian J. Frank Dobie, with the intention of fortifying a robust regional culture.

Regional architecture, entrenched in physical and cultural examination, represented a return to basics. Ford's architectural designs celebrated the particulars of place with native Texas materials, thick walls, metal roofs, courtyards, patios, dog trots, trellises, and arbors. After he and Williams went their separate ways in 1932, Ford's client list grew to include Frank Murchison for whom he designed a modern house in San Antonio (considered the first in the state), and Sid Richardson for whom he designed a low and linear vacation house near Corpus Christi. By 1938 Ford was starting to work, with his partner Arch Swank, on the Little Chapel in the Woods which, as its name implies, is small in scale for an ecclesiastic structure. Ford and Swank made it awe-inspiring by basing the structure on a series of 30-foot tall parabolic arches. By the time these three projects were completed, Ford was considered Texas' foremost modernist architect.

Ford came to San Antonio at the invitation of David Williams to consult on the restoration of La Villita, an assemblage of eighteenth- and nineteenth-century buildings overlooking the San Antonio River. After World War II, Ford and partner Jerry Rogers opened an office at Willow Way, an architecturally eccentric compound near Mission San Jose that included a main house, sheds, and a few cottages. Ford's office was also his home, and there he mentored and nurtured a large group of employees whom he considered family. It was also during this period that he began a forty-year relationship with Trinity University, designing the new campus on an abandoned quarry north of downtown. In 1966 he joined Boone Powell and Chris Carson in the eponymous firm Ford Powell & Carson that thrives today. That office cultivated younger architects, such as Ted Flato and David Lake, who opened their San Antonio firm in 1984. Lake|Flato has become one of the country's most eloquent evangelists of regionalism.

The genealogy of architects who continue to carry out the principles of site-specific design championed by O'Neil Ford is a clear one. Another generation of architects has spun off from the Lake|Flato firm, including Tobin Smith. Dallas-based architect Max Levy (2017 recipient of the O'Neil Ford medal for design achievement) is one of the few Ford acolytes still practicing. That group also included Frank Welch before his death in June 2017. Bentley Tibbs considers himself Welch's protégé. Larry Speck, an ardent proponent of regionalism and fan of the Dallas modernist Bud Oglesby, has written and spoken often on the topic.

What is Texan about the houses featured in this book is a pervading sense of place, deeply embedded in tangible realities—history, climate, topography, traditions, the economy, and the culture. They represent an authentic vision of what Texas is. More than anything *Texas Made/Texas Modern* is about identity—our own, of course, but in a broader sense, our identity as dwellers in a unique part of the world. The book is filled with discerning images of nineteen Texas houses by architectural photographer Casey Dunn. His photographs reveal how architects, interior designers, and their clients have defined place in the environment. It's been up to us to notice it, to understand it, and to build our houses accordingly, so that we know where we are in time, in location, and in the natural order of things. That is what regional architecture does for us. That is also why, when you look at these houses, you know that their architecture, their siting, and the way they address their environment means only one thing: there is no other place these houses can be other than where they are—in Texas.

# THINGS SEEN AND UNSEEN

MILL SPRING, TEXAS

LAKE|FLATO ARCHITECTS

**Preceding spread and opposite:** A jagged path of concrete pavers set between the lawn and the garden leads to the entry steps below the house. The rear elevation reveals the basic materials: copper roof and Leuders limestone walls with horizontal wood siding. The copper will patinate to green over time.

It is usually assumed that the site makes a house. But in the case of this steel, limestone, and glass dwelling near Vanderpool, the meandering structure engages with the site so expressively that the setting became more irresistible than it had been before the house was built. The property, on the Edwards Plateau, was a working ranch when the current owners bought it. "We chose a site between two small creeks so that they could be near shade and cooling water," Lake|Flato project architect Steve Raike explains. Topography aside, the architects thought the most evocative part of the site was a rugged fifty-year-old poured-in-place concrete dam, built as a way to collect water for the cattle on the ranch. "It felt like an ancient artifact to us," says Raike. "We decided to treat it like a revered object and build the house just off the dam."

The 4,300-square-foot, four-structure complex sits at the water's edge beside the dam where the two streams converge. Three of the four buildings—the main house with living and dining areas, and the two guest houses—are composed of rough-back Lueders limestone with steel-and-glass walls as a counterpoint. Their light-as-air transparency contrasts with the massive walls, offering a dynamic of openness that interacts with the protective presence of the massive walls. A concrete storage building serves double duty with parking on top. "The owners and their guests leave their cars there, abandoning all the things that brought them here before they enter the sheltering enclosure," says Raike.

The buildings surround a courtyard shaded by mature pecan and cypress trees that landscape architect Christy Ten Eyck wove through the compound. Views from the house open to the courtyard and onto the creeks, but other spaces contemplate the valley.

Rooms also unfold, courtesy of glass walls that roll back to create a continuous series of open spaces. At one end of the main building, the living room opens onto a cantilevered deck that seems to fly over the creek; on the other end, walls slide back to connect the room with grassy terraces and concrete steps that float down to the dam. These strategies ensure that the buildings use only natural ventilation except in extreme conditions, when a geothermal HVAC system takes over. But, even when the temperature soars, the architecture—which feels both open and sheltering—encourages a sense of cooling calm. The stone takes the brunt of the Texas heat, but the play of light and the sound of water are ethereal elements of the construction. Here, water always entices, a fulfillment of an invitation accepted by the architects to make nature even better than it was when they started.

In the living area, soaring, asymmetrically pitched ceilings are composed of white oak panels underneath Douglas fir beams, all supported by steel beams. A yellow occasional table designed by Laura Kirar is placed between a Contempo leather sectional and swivel chairs by Poltrona Frau.

**Opposite and above:** Contemporary club chairs form a convivial grouping in front of the living room fireplace. The corner window seat offers a more secluded spot. **Right:** Steps lead down from the living room to the swimming porch overlooking the pool.

**Right:** Sliding doors roll back to open the living room entirely to the outside. The swimming porch floor is concrete—as is the bridge across the creek. While the concrete was wet, depressions were imprinted into a gridded pattern on the concrete slabs and filled with aggregate so that the areas are slip resistant. **Overleaf:** In the evening, the geometry and transparency of the house are revealed.

# UPLIFTED

LLANO, TEXAS

MICHAEL HSU OFFICE OF ARCHITECTURE

**Preceding spread:** The entrance court is defined by projecting wings, the master bedroom on the right and the garage on the left. **Opposite:** The living room ceiling panels are pine and fir. Trim—including the panels on the steel staircase—is white oak with a wax finish, and some of the furniture is mesquite. Interior designer Laura Roberts designed the angular coffee table, made locally from a single chunk of wood.

"Once this house was finished," says Bart Knaggs, "the impact was profound and unexpected."

The fact that the owner was surprised by the glass, wood, and rock weekend getaway architect Michael Hsu designed for him and his family is something of a surprise in itself. Knaggs, an irrepressible entrepreneur, is a partner in a hospitality company that has developed a half-dozen or so restaurants in Austin. He is partial to cutting-edge style, but he elicits from architects a frisson of newness that invests buildings with a sense of belonging, whether the neighborhood is old or new. Or, in the case of this family weekend house in Llano, when the neighborhood is geographically unique.

Knaggs and his wife, Barbara, a school teacher and an expert in public policy, had long nurtured the idea of having a house on their property overlooking the Llano River. Because he is a modernist, Hsu wasn't an obvious choice for a country house. But the architect works beyond glass-box predictability, endowing each of his projects with a unique sense of place. "We don't talk about architecture as shape and mass," says Hsu. "Instead we ask, 'What is the mood, what is the atmosphere?'" The answer to those questions is measured qualitatively with an architectural gesture, with lighting, and with materials.

By the time Hsu began to sketch, he and his client had spent countless hours on the property. "We'd paddle around in the canoe, do some fishing, and talk about the place," says Knaggs. "I wanted a house that was quiet and tactile, but also impervious and robust." But most of all he wanted the family to be able to experience the outdoors, especially while they were inside. Hsu designed the 3,200-square-foot house to offer all of that. A double-height glass box allows for star-gazing. The living, dining, and kitchen share a downstairs space that opens onto a concrete porch where another kitchen is set up. Upstairs, glass walls in the children's lofts let them view the stars in the night sky—just as they did when the family camped out on the property before the house was built. One wing houses the master bedroom, cloaked in tight-jointed dry-stack weathered limestone sourced nearby. On the other side, a garage is sided with barn doors so that the family can easily drag their eight canoes and kayaks in and out.

The approach to the house is part of the experience. The two-hour drive from Austin establishes the distance between big city and country getaway. But it's the turn off the highway onto Lower Willow Creek Road that signals something special. "I stop there and roll down the window," says Kragss. "When the car crosses the cattle guard, the rattling sound it makes and the sound of the tires on the dirt road gets my head right. I'm at my place and I'm ready to be there. That's what the architecture did for us—and I wasn't expecting that."

**Above:** The stairwell is framed by a white plaster box. **Opposite:** The custom walnut dining table has a live edge and was made by Austin-based Hewn fabricators. The dining chairs are upholstered in vintage military tents dyed indigo. **Opposite, below:** The underside of the stair encloses storage and display space. The built-in sectional was designed by Joe Zambarano.

**Opposite:** In the family room, two leather butterfly chairs face a coffee table fashioned with an old stone top and reclaimed teak balls. Floors are polished concrete. **Above:** Barn doors slide back to reveal a tackle room lined with shou sugi ban wood panels. **Overleaf:** The Knaggs family camped out on this site for years before the house was built. The fire pit is a tribute to the many nights they spent in front of a camp fire.

# URBAN OUTLOOK

DALLAS, TEXAS

MAX LEVY ARCHITECT

Deborah Orrill was driving down Royal Lane in Dallas one day when she noticed a sign announcing Urban Reserve, an award-winning development that's the brain child of developer Diane Cheatham. Buying a new house was the last thing on the culinary consultant's mind, though. She and her husband, Blair Sanders, the former director of cloud technology for Xerox, had lived in the same house for thirty years, and they were thinking, instead, how nice it would be to very soon have a paid-off mortgage.

But the couple was intrigued. She and Sanders thought that they might not get a bigger house, but that they could get a better one to replace their current inward-looking tract house built around a courtyard. They considered what was possible and concluded that they might as well upend everything about their lives. Sanders and Orill bought a lot and interviewed four architects Urban Reserve recommended, one of whom was Max Levy. Levy is a native Texan and a modernist, known for connecting houses with nature in poetic, cost-effective ways.

The couple's lot is triangular, with an acute angle at one end too tight for a house or even a part of a house, to squeeze itself into. Levy arrived at a clever solution. He broke what was to be a 2,500-square-foot house into two 16-foot-wide rectangles—a 50-foot-long structure for the garage with two bedrooms over it and a 60-foot-long, one-story unit to accommodate the main living area. A corner of that building is nudged underneath the eaves of the bedroom wing. Levy then added a two-story metal-clad cylinder in the tip end of the triangle. "It was a way to use as much of the site as we could," the architect says. "The cylinder is a lovely form and slipping it into the end of the "V" was a bit like fitting a toe into Cinderella's slipper."

It was about this time that Levy began to wonder about a subject that had never been mentioned. Deborah Orrill is a nationally known culinary expert and Levy assumed she'd have some imperatives to make about the appearance of the kitchen. But Orrill held off, for good reasons. "I went to cooking school in France, and they teach you how to do everything manually," she explains. She wanted to keep things simple, and Levy accommodated with a galley kitchen overlooked by a bank of floor-to-ceiling windows.

The house has lived up to, if not surpassed, the owners' original intent. Sanders and Orrill have been beguiled by the sunrises and sunsets, as well as by the paths of the moon. From the martini deck atop the entry cylinder, the world is spread out at their feet. "We can see the bike path, Royal Oaks golf course, and some of the Dallas skyline," says Sanders. The smaller world beckons too: shadows on the walls and rain rattling on the galvanized metal roof are endlessly interesting. "This house has given us a way to interact with nature that we never had before," says Sanders. "It keeps amazing us."

The silo shape is a prominent feature of the design, both as a rain collection system on the deck just outside the kitchen and as the entry to the house.

Les Orientalistes
BIRD

**Preceding spread:** In the living room, oversize windows are supported by LVL laminated veneer studs that were already part of the infrastructure. The peripatetic owners purchased the Poltrona Frau sofa and Mies chairs when they lived in Europe. **Above and opposite:** The 10-foot-high ceiling is painted dark gray to extend the visual perception of space to the outside. A Noguchi pendant hangs above the dining table, custom by Jason David Smith, who also designed the cabinetry.

The 30-foot-long galley-style kitchen is divided into a front kitchen and a back kitchen, hidden behind a wall at the far end of the counter. Tucked behind the wall are cabinets, an oven, and space to stage meals. The open kitchen is separated from the living room by a misty-blue wall where Orrill hangs her copper pots and pans, a tribute to Julia Child's uber-practical pegboard system where she hung utensils in plain sight.

MATISSE

# CLIFFHANGER

AUSTIN, TEXAS

POLLEN ARCHITECTURE & DESIGN

"This is very much a case study kind of house," says architect Elizabeth Alford about the rock-and-cypress house tucked away on a hilly street in Austin. She and her husband, artist Michael Young, and their two children live in the late 1950s house. Their street is on the Balcones fault zone, the geographical boundary between the prairie lands that extends from the Gulf of Mexico to the craggy Texas Hill Country; its tell-tale fractures in the topography are all around the Alford-Young house.

The couple, who own Pollen Architecture & Design along with their business partner architect Dason Whitsett, moved into the 1,500-square-foot house with the intention of renovating it. The house, designed by Austin architect Jonathan Bowman, was a gem-like symbol of an exuberant period in the city's architectural history, displaying the characteristics other midcentury houses in that rugged area of the city share—small in scale and economically built.

But the house also exuded optimism in a big way, reflecting the enthusiasm for the modernist movement that had found its way into Austin via architects such as Harwell Hamilton Harris, who had apprenticed with Richard Neutra. From 1952 to1955 Harris was dean of the School of Architecture at the University of Texas and attracted like-minded architects to the faculty. "I love this era in Austin," says Alford. "The houses show an appreciation for modernism while fitting into the Texas landscape." It represented an intersection of a progressive strain of Texan identity with the land and the topography.

Other aspects of the house—including sagging exposed wood beams and inadequate insulation—drove the couple's decision to take the modest dwelling down to the slab. Or almost to the slab. Still remaining are two elements that gave the house its Texas-tough personality in the first place: the limestone rock foundation and the central stairwell that leads from the ground-level carport up to the main living area. The ingenious stairwell acts as a thermal chimney. "There's always a little puff of air right there," says Alford.

Alford and Young added 1,000 square feet, using local materials, like aggregate dredged from the Trinity River that was mixed with concrete and then polished for a personal version of terrazzo. The placement of windows was guided as much by the sun's angles as by catching the views. South- and west-facing window banks are fitted with awnings that shade the rooms during the heat of the day, while clerestory windows reflect natural light onto the family room ceiling. The more obvious window in the room, though, is the folding glass wall that slides open and shut like an accordion. It opens the room to the patio, an ever-present invitation to go outside without using the conventional route through a doorway.

Quarter-sawn East Texas yellow pine, cut to reveal an inherent pattern of horizontal lines, covers much of the walls, doors, ceilings and soffits, and some of the floors in public areas of the house. Fleetwood rolling glass doors extend the length of the room. Alford and Young designed the bright yellow MDF credenza, the backdrop for the two vintage modular Dieter Rams 620 Chair Programme chairs.

**Above:** Young often incorporates sand and soil into his work, as seen in the large-scale piece hanging in the dining area. A pendant lamp with a collapsible silicone shade by Swedish designers Form Us with Love for Muuto hangs above the locally made Macek Furniture Company dining table. **Opposite:** In the stairwell, the finely striated concrete tile wall contrasts with the rough limestone rock of the original stair column.

MATISSE
The Art of East Asia

**Opposite:** Strategically placed clerestory windows at the junction of the butterfly roof reflect natural light into the interior. Aggregate dredged from the Trinity River bottom is mixed with concrete for floors that evoke the world outside. **Above and right:** The son's bedroom furniture is custom by Hatch Workshop. Walls encourage hanging special mementoes and art.

From the carport below, visitors walk underneath the main volume of the house and then ascend stairs to the living spaces, which overlook hills, a canopy of trees, and a lush ravine. The facade of the balcony over the carport is cypress washed with a translucent gray stain.

# CULTURED CLUB

DALLAS, TEXAS

BODRON + FRUIT

**Preceding spread:** The owners furnished the living room with pieces from their former house, also designed by Bodron+Fruit. The Dunbar coffee table with mosaic pull-outs belonged to the owner's grandmother. **Opposite:** A painting by Jerry Bywaters hangs in the entry, the current owners' tribute to the original owner of the house. A closet in the brick wall that faced the front door was replaced with a floating brick wall that opens up the space visually. All the pink brick is original.

The late 1920s and early 1930s was a heady time in the development of ideas about regional architecture in Texas. After a trip through the state with his protégé O'Neil Ford, architect David Williams described a new kind of architecture in a 1931 article for the influential *Southwest Review:*

> A logical regional architecture has for its origin the simple, early forms of building native to its own locale, and grows by purely functional methods into an indigenous form of art . . . this style is modern, for it satisfies all the requirements of modern design and construction.

Williams and Ford were at the center of a bohemian intellectual elite in Dallas that included artists, architects, writers, actors, and professors. All were robust proponents of the belief that art—if it was to be significant—had to be a reflection of life where you were living it. Some of these thinkers and doers ended up commissioning houses in a then-rural part of Dallas near Southern Methodist University that American folklorist J. Frank Dobie dubbed "Culture Gulch." The houses were all built facing a pond just where Turtle Creek begins, and the modest red-brick residence that Ford designed for artist and director of the Dallas Museum of Art Jerry Bywaters still stands. Historian Lon Tinkle and his wife, Maria, built a house (now demolished) across the pond; the Bywaters and Tinkle children shuttled between houses in row boats.

The Bywaters house lives on, thanks to a sensitive renovation by new owners under the curation of interior designer Mil Bodron and architect Svend Fruit of the firm Bodron+Fruit. When the house went on the market in 2007, the current owner and Mil Bodron couldn't resist walking through it. "We assumed it would be a tear-down," Bodron says. "My client had no intention of buying it, but once we got inside, we saw the potential. It was a little jewel."

Many of Ford's houses were rambling forms, but this one was economical in style. From the street, it appeared to be horizontal, but at the rear, the profile of the wedge-shaped house shadows the curving profile of the pond. "He was still experimenting with what he wanted to do with modernism," says Bodron. So as not to detract from the dwelling's effortless harmony with nature, Fruit and Bodron devised a wing for each end of the house—two new bedrooms for the children at one end and a new master bedroom at the other. They also added a porch and enclosed a screened porch with glass for use as the dining room. "We gave every room in the additions a view twelve feet down to the creek," notes Fruit. Site and house are inextricably entwined, as if one can't exist without the other. That was Ford's intention. "It's not until you are inside the house that you understand the site," says the owner. "That's when you can see how perfectly situated the house is."

A narrow marble frame serves as a bar counter and a divider between the kitchen and the breakfast room. On the white hall wall is Laura Wilson's photograph of Donald Judd.

The wood-and-glass doors to the dining room are the original exterior doors to what was once a screened porch. The generous space perfectly accommodates the owner's extra-long Edward Wormley for Dunbar dining table and chairs, which belonged to her grandmother.

DALLAS MODERN
Sheila Hicks 50 Years
MARK ROTHKO
VREELAND MEMOS

**Opposite:** New exterior walls for the addition, visible in the courtyard between a sitting room and the master bedroom, are stained Douglas fir. The courtyard marks the end of the original house and the beginning of the addition. **Above:** The master bedroom is part of one of two new wings that flank the original house.

Gravel-filled poured-in-place concrete steps lead down to a small lake below the house. Landscaping is by Mary Ellen Cowan of MESA.

# COOL, CALM, AND COLLECTED

WIMBERLEY, TEXAS

MARCUS MOHON INTERIORS

"Modern is an attitude," says Austin-based designer Marcus Mohon. His philosophy is elegantly expressed in a renovation of a 1970s ranch house on the Blanco River in the Texas Hill Country. Both traditional and minimal, the house is a testament to the off-beat magic that happens when an interior designer and a savvy client collaborate. But his remark about the nature of "modern" reveals his very specific intentions for the house. "The Saarinen Tulip table is the only modern piece," he says. The table is an icon of modern design and its prominent placement in the middle of the living space, serves to clarify—if not define—all other objects in the room.

"This was a casual process," Mohon observes, commenting on his dual role as architect and interior designer. The kitchen was gutted, and removing a wall connected the new two-island kitchen with the dining and living rooms. Two bunkrooms that sleep six each and two baths were added at the end of the house next to the game room, increasing the living space to 3,500 square feet. Mohon extended an existing porch to open the long and lean house to the view of the river and the cypresses along its banks. Steel sliding doors replaced windows for easy indoor-outdoor access and act as giant frames for the natural wonders beyond. With sliding doors on either side of the house, it only takes opening them all up to turn the main body of the house into a big, happy breezeway.

As for decor, indestructibility was guaranteed because everything in the house has already stood the test of time. The owner attends the Round Top Antiques Fair, often multiple times a season. She has filled a barn on the family property with furniture and accessories so all Mohon had to do was get in his truck and drive over to pick out vintage chairs, light fixtures, cow hides, and other decorative objects. The effect is richly textured and interesting. Since most of the items have endured for years out, their longevity had already been tested, and they stylishly fulfill the owner's mandate for durability. The eccentric array also satisfies the designer's mission to create a space with pieces that assert their singularity as icons, whether they have been acknowledged as such or not.

rome home
PERFECT BATH BARBARA SALLICK

The ladder, the two rush-backed chairs, the cowhide rugs, the wood chest of drawers, and the black-and-white primitive/modern painting are all part of the owner's stockpile of pieces from the Round Top Antiques Fair.

**Right:** Mohon chose not to hang much art in this house, preferring instead to focus on the view of the Blanco River. For the living room, the designer repurposed an A. Rudin leather chair from the owners' in-town house. The coffee table and petrified wood side table are Round Top finds. Mohon added the chunky cedar support posts on the porch. **Overleaf:** The game room was once the garage, but it has been refurbished as a theater for watching movies, with tiered platforms padded with cushions, bolsters, and pillows.

**Above:** In the kitchen, there are two Caesarstone-topped islands, one for food preparation and the other for eating. **Opposite:** The vertical bead board in the dining room is a backdrop for a ladder hung horizontally on the wall. The Saarinen table is paired with a Mexican leather barrel chair and lit by two Mercury glass lamps on pedestals.

The grill-like base on the lamps in the guest room resembles an assemblage of cattle brands, as do the pictograph-style markings on the textile hanging behind the bed. To make the bedrooms larger, all the closets were removed and benches added for suitcases and lots of hooks for hanging things up.

# SPEAK TO ME

LOST PINES, TEXAS

HUGH JEFFERSON RANDOLPH ARCHITECTS

**Preceding spread and opposite:** The two-bedroom bunkhouse, clad in weathered cedar siding, is connected to the main house by a deep porch. The front entry the main house is unpainted stucco topped by a black-and-white awning; it's flanked by two wings faced in hand-pressed bricks from Mexico.

When Gina and Bill O'Hara approached Austin-based architect Hugh Randolph about designing a house in the country near Bastrop's Lost Pines, Gina arrived at the architect's office with thirteen pages of notes that included her ideas for the overall feel of the house, dimensions of the rooms, and the finishes. "I told Hugh I wanted a house that looked like the one in *Out of Africa*," she explains. Karen Blixen's stone house with red metal roof, bay windows, and wide verandas was Gina's idea of a house whose authenticity of materials endowed it with weight and meaning. She didn't want a replica of the house, but she used the reference as a way to communicate her ideas to her husband and to the architect.

"Not everything about site-specific architecture is physical," Randolph observes. "Pragmatism and dreaming affect how buildings end up looking." The O'Haras' L-shaped house is two long and skinny structures, set at a 90-degree angle to each other to create a courtyard where Gina has developed elaborate gardens. The main house is brick and stucco with steel gridded windows and a metal roof. The other structure, which houses the garage and two guest rooms, is more casual, with wood siding and painted trim. Each building has its own wide veranda, which merge at the junction of the two buildings. The brick, wood, and rock telegraph a message that was important to Gina. "I realized that every house I like is composed of materials that have a certain weight," she says. She chose materials—such as concrete for the floors, American Clay (a natural earth plaster product) for most of the walls, and shiplap for other walls—that convey authenticity. "It gives the house a certain feeling, but I don't think that people usually break down emotionally what leads to that. It's just there."

The O'Hara house is on the Colorado River, in a part of the state that is a geological anomaly—just past the edge of the Hill Country where it verges into the very westernmost selvedge of the Piney Woods, a 13-mile non-continuous population of trees. They are separated, but closely related genetically, to the vast expanse of pine trees of the Piney Woods region that covers parts of East Texas, Arkansas, Louisiana, and Oklahoma. "This is a river bottom," Gina says, noting that the old farmland suits her gardening avocation. "I started thinking about the house with one thing I loved, the Moroccan-style tiles now in the kitchen," she says, "and then I planned one thing after the next." Everything in the house has the mark of personality, thoughtfully researched and sought after, carefully installed and displayed, and savored as only a loving connoisseur can. "It's not a fancy house," the owner suggests, "but it has a good feeling to it."

The O'Haras chose to paint the walls in the main house with American Clay, a natural earth product with a plaster-like finish. The living room walls are the same hand-pressed bricks used on the exterior. Floors are polished concrete; overhead, rough-hewn beams are reclaimed wood.

**Opposite:** The stenciled tile in the kitchen occupies one wall, creating the effect of a mural. The beams overhead are reclaimed, and the light fixtures are some of the many that Gina O'Hara—a vintage lighting enthusiast—has collected. **Above and right:** In the master bathroom, a vintage tub sits in a bay window. To the right is a door that opens into the garden. **Overleaf:** The patio in front of the house is composed of pea gravel, Lueders limestone slabs, and hand-pressed Mexican brick. Gina built the stacked stone walls herself from rock sourced from their property. The garden is planted with poppies, bluebonnets, prairie verbena, and mealy blue sage.

# SITE SPECIFIC

DALLAS, TEXAS

LAWRENCE W. SPECK

Architect Lawrence Speck is an admirer of the work of the late Dallas-based modernist Bud Oglesby. So when a newly widowed friend asked if he would take a look at a recent purchase—a 6,000-square-foot Oglesby house built in the 1970s—Speck agreed to make the trip from Austin to Dallas to see it. What he found was a two-story house in poor condition, an obvious candidate for bull-dozing. But there was one saving grace, and it was one common to all Oglesby designs: the house was beautifully sited. The low-slung dwelling sat at a diagonal to a tree-lined street that terminates at the bank of the meandering Turtle Creek. "Bud was a master at the way he placed houses in a natural setting," notes the owner's friend and interior designer, Emily Summers.

When Speck—the former dean of the University of Texas School of Architecture and now a principal at the well-known architectural firm Page—walked through the residence, he was reminded of Oglesby's typical approach of clustering service spaces—closets, baths, and stairways—in the core of the structure so that exterior walls accommodate big windows and big views. For some reason, that strategy was not used in this house. The views into the lush waterway had been truncated, virtually eliminating enjoyment of the natural setting. Speck felt that the windows were the problem: "The house needed to open to the creek, where the magic is."

The architect took on the assignment of restoring life to the house, and in some cases reinventing it. Speck redesigned both ends, creating glass wings that welcomed views of the verdant bend in Turtle Creek. He also designed a multi-story suspended glass-and-steel curtain wall that encloses the living room, study, and master bedroom. The middle of the house remained intact as did the roofline and the profile. It was if Speck was conducting a dialogue about the balance of mass (the Oglesby conversation) and transparency (Speck's contribution).

From that point on, both architecture and interior design revolved around refining the residence. It was clad in sand-blasted Texas limestone and Almendrillo wood siding and topped with a custom copper Bermuda-shingle roof, textural materials that entwined the interior with the exterior. Because the owner entertains frequently, furniture was selected that would endure large gatherings.

In many ways, this renovation project achieved maximum effect for all involved. Speck was able to rethink the positive aspects of the house, extracting the best of Bud Oglesby's intentions and elaborating on them. For Emily Summers, the project offered the chance to help one of her oldest friends move into a new life. And Speck, who focuses mainly on civic and commercial projects, was energized by the domestic project. In this house Speck provided the owner not just with a place to put an address on, but with a place worthy of a new beginning. For both architect and interior designer, this project was energized by a double opportunity—to breathe life into an admired colleague's design and to give a dear friend a place worthy of a new beginning.

**Preceding spread:** Multilayered organza sheers filter light in the master bedroom where the sculptural lines of a vintage Vladimir Kagan chaise on a brass stand invite repose. **Left:** Designer Emily Summers specified cream-colored Grasello plaster walls and ceilings throughout the house; the material has an inherent luminescence that bathes each room in soft translucence. In the kitchen, white Bulthaup cabinetry achieves the same illuminating effect, softened by the matte-finished quarter-sawn oak floors. The kitchen and family room open onto a patio and the backyard beyond.

**Opposite:** A white lacquer table in the dining room seats twelve; a round table in the entry hall is used when extra seating is needed. Ceramic ribbons are installed on a white-oak wall separating the kitchen and dining room, a nod to the owner's love of pottery. **Above:** An etched-glass panel at the entry provides privacy. Beyond the entry and dining room, the patio offers more capacity for guests.

Emily Summers undertook an international search for furniture, finding coffee tables in Paris and arm chairs in Shanghai. She also designed custom pieces such as the sofas and club chairs for the living room. To gain a full view of the wooded setting, architects Larry Speck and Jason Smith designed a suspended curtain-wall of steel and glass that encloses the living room, office, and master bedroom on the second floor.

**Opposite:** A gold-leaf screen acquired in Kyoto sits on a credenza in the office, where floor-to-ceiling windows offer an unobstructed view. **Above:** A niche in the master bedroom displays pieces from the owner's collection of ceramics. **Overleaf:** Speck retained the original vocabulary of natural materials but upgraded them, opting for sandblasted Lueders limestone sawn to lock into a running bond with long thin units and a copper roof to replace shingles. Mary Ellen Cowan of MESA created a modern template for the yard, extending the patio to the back yard with Lueders limestone platforms that arrive at a pea gravel landing.

# REMEMBRANCE OF THINGS PAST

AUSTIN, TEXAS

PAUL LAMB ARCHITECTS

Architect Paul Lamb has been in Austin for thirty years, long enough to recall the city's halcyon days of the 1950s and 1960s. At that time, the hills west of Austin, dense with cedar trees and sliced through by winding gravel roads, were enticingly close to town but fostered a feeling of remoteness. It was a favorite place for the more bohemian professors at the University of Texas, particularly those in the art department, to live and work. Some built their own houses in this woodsy redoubt; others renovated. These dwellings were idiosyncratic, earthy, and rambling. A few were modern.

When Janet and Wilson Allen commissioned Lamb to design a house for them and their three children in Westlake Hills, that whisper of local lore informed Lamb's intuition about what the Allen house could feel like—casual, imaginative, and a place where life is lived to the fullest. "The site is powerful," says Lamb. "Materials can be robust, and we have room to breathe." He envisioned the 5,500-square-foot reclaimed barnwood and glass house as tough and sophisticated.

Nestled into a slope, the house faces a sweeping view of the Austin skyline. The approach is leisurely, through a low-ceilinged loggia supported on the sides by eight reclaimed long-leaf yellow pine columns that terminates at the house. To the right is a two-story screened porch accessible via a staircase. Ahead modern French doors open onto an inner courtyard anchored by a double-height stacked fieldstone fireplace and limestone terrace. To the left of the loggia is the main entry into the public spaces of the house, an open living area that includes the living room, the family room, the dining area, and the kitchen.

Wilson Allen wanted a kitchen where he could flip pancakes right out onto the table where his kids gather for breakfast. But the farmhouse-style kitchen is also in full view of the living and dining rooms so the hipped-ceiling space expresses the easy-going dressiness that interior designer Susan Ferrier bestowed on the entire house. Lamb accommodated the father's request with a live-edge chestnut slab as the table and placed the stove out of view at the end (handy for pancake-flipping onto awaiting plates). The bar-height slab is supported by part of one of the loggia's reclaimed long leaf yellow pine columns and is flanked by four linen-slipcovered chairs. An adjacent shiplap-paneled dining space with banquette seating at a steel-topped table easily converts from a favorite homework outpost to formal dining. Best of all, the kitchen window offers the finest perspective in the house—a panoramic vista of the Austin skyline. Lamb's rationale is informed by respect for the landscape, the setting that invests the house with a reason for being. "Why not give the most-used room in the house the best view?" he says.

**Preceding spread and right:** Architect Paul Lamb found old barn wood (with flecks of the original red and white paint still visible) to use as siding, pairing it with stacked sandstone walls. The wall continues into a two-story tall screened porch adjacent to the patio and terracing that steps into landscaping by Dylan Crain. The house is built around a Lueders limestone patio and centered on a sandstone fireplace that uses the same chimney as the living room fireplace one story above. Crain added the skeletal tree next to the fireplace, which has remained in place as a sculptural statement.

A row of clerestory windows spreads the north light throughout the living room. The beams are fir; ceiling panels are Alaskan yellow cedar. A wall sculpture by James Surls hangs on the sandstone fireplace.

A seating area is separated from the adjacent living room by a curtain wall, a Susan Ferrier signature element. Interior walls are painted poplar. Another curtain wall defines the entry hall; just beyond it barn doors slide shut to conceal an office.

**Opposite:** The owners didn't want a formal dining room, opting for banquette seating and a table in an eating area next to the kitchen. Floors throughout are reclaimed white oak. **Above:** A reclaimed longleaf yellow pine column supports the kitchen table, a visual connection to the columns that frame the loggia at the front of the house. Lamb emphasizes an ad hoc attitude with the slanted roof made to suggest a porch ceiling with an add-on flat ceiling over windows with the best view in the house.

# VIEWFINDER

HENLY, TEXAS

LEMMO ARCHITECTURE AND DESIGN

Long before David and Kathy Clem bought their Hill Country ranch—and long before David began hiking its craggy thousand acres and looking for a place to build a writing studio—deer and other wildlife had already trod a path along a limestone cliff that overlooks the river running through the property. The ready-made trail alerted David, a developer who specializes in sustainable projects in and around Boston, that the cliff edge didn't just offer an efficient way for deer and elk to get from one end to the other. Spread out before it was one of the most spectacular panoramas on the ranch. It was a prospect that existed solely from that special place where the topography plunges to the river.

The margin of the precipice is where David chose to site the writing studio and hunting blind he planned to build. The idea of the building—and the remoteness—appealed to Ryan and Stephanie Lemmo, the architects hired to design the two steel boxes he envisioned. "You have to drive through four cattle gates and then snake around a big field of winter oats and drive down a caliche road for about fifteen minutes before you arrive at the site," says Ryan. The rocky landscape became the driving force in the design of the pair of Cor-Ten boxes connected by a breezeway that would constitute David Clem's retreat.

The process was slow going. "It took me five years to understand this property," says David. "It was infested with cedars, and clearing the land was a long-term process." While the goal was to take the land back to its original state, he wanted something cutting-edge for his private getaway. "I wanted to create something modernist," he says. "I knew I wanted it made out of steel." His reasons were infused with nostalgia as well as with admiration for modern design. The steel was a loving reference to his father who built oil field tanks in Tyler, Texas, where both David and Kathy grew up. David and his father also used to hunt together, and although David has never actually fired a shot from the blind now that it's built, the structure is symbolic of an experience that bonded him with his father.

With the help of construction manager Ron Reue, Ryan and Stephanie Lemmo addressed the vocabulary that David had specified. From the entry at the lip of the cliff, the structure is inconspicuous. The building is designed so that visitors engage with it from the moment of arrival at the rusted steel-and-hog-wire stairs that lead over the breezeway and around the writing studio. The wrap-around staircase eventually emerges at the lower level, but en route it allows different vantage points to enjoy the landscape. Once inside, each room is fronted with a wall of glass that exposes the grandeur of the topography.

The two volumes of the hunting blind/writing studio are connected by stairs that ascend in a leisurely route around the buildings. One is topped with a roof terrace; the other with a rocky fill that further ties the building to the landscape. Entry is from the top, at the edge of a limestone cliff, via a bridge above a breezeway. The bridge turns left, wraps around the hunting blind component of the buildings before descending under the bridge to a dog trot between the structures.

Building elements inside and out are just as utilitarian as the structural components of the two buildings. The stair, deck, and bridge railings are ungalvanized hog wire 4-by-4-inch panels topped with ipe; stair flooring is raw steel bar grating. All are supported by steel I-beams. Inside the writing studio, the ceiling is locally sourced pecan, and walls are upholstered with hemasote, a burlap wrap often used in design schools for inspiration boards that also has acoustic properties the Clemms value.

# ROCK SOLID

UVALDE, TEXAS

LAKE|FLATO ARCHITECTS

When this couple decided to retire from their professional lives in New York, they were determined to return to the wife's family land on a wooded bluff twenty-five miles from Uvalde, Texas. Since the mid-1980s, the couple had frequently visited the 500-acre property to hunt pheasant and to luxuriate in the welcome provided by a grove of mature oaks, outcroppings of Texas sage, wildlife galore, and birds passing through on their migrations. The crystal-clear Nueces River cuts through the property too. "I love the weather here," says the wife, noting a phenomenon that belies its location at the verge of West Texas. Thanks to an elevation of nearly 1,000 feet on the Edwards Plateau, humidity is lower and nights are cooler than in the central part of the state.

The owners were specific about the house they intended to build: "We wanted a house that fit the landscape." They also wanted the house to be discreet, as if it was peeking out of the landscape. "And," says the wife, "we planned to use someone local." Ordinarily, finding an architect in a remote part of Texas would have been a challenge, but when they began researching, the couple found that Lake|Flato was only eighty miles away in San Antonio.

Although the owners had already picked out a site, when Ted Flato and firm partner Karla Greer arrived with topographical maps in hand, all four hiked the land. "Ted was like a water diviner," says the owner. "He looked at the map and said, 'Take me here.'" "Here" was a piece of untouched property neither owner had ever seen before despite having explored the area for years. It was perfect, on a bluff where there are constant breezes and behind a row of oaks.

The design began with the owners specifying how many rooms they needed. The resulting 2,600-square-foot house is a long stretch of locally sourced limestone, copper, steel, and glass. "We reinterpreted the simple shed structure," says project architect Rebecca Comeaux. Two pavilions at one end are topped with shed roofs that cover a porch and living room of matching size; a boxy volume houses the kitchen; and another shed-topped pavilion butts up to it where the master bedroom is.

The architecture makes the owners feel as if they are outside even when they aren't. The floor-to-ceiling steel-framed glass windows flank the limestone fireplace in the living room, suggesting that this space is open-air, just as its companion porch actually is in the open. "I am out there about 75 percent of the time," says the owner who reads, dines, and spends an occasional night in the space.

Since the house was completed, the homeowners have added a deck on the roof above the kitchen. It's in use now as a place for star-gazing. "But we are ready for the eclipse on April 8, 2024," says the husband. "The sun will be passing right over us."

Sandblasted Lueders limestone slabs, cut at random lengths, are used for the walls throughout the house in response to the owners' preference for rough, matte surfaces. In the kitchen, cabinets were built from white-oak boards, fumed to give the boards a richer color. The owners furnished the house with family heirlooms and comfortable seating.

The entry arbor is covered with fragrant white Lady Banks climbing roses. Christy Ten Eyck of Ten Eyck Landscape Architects planted native, drought-tolerant plants throughout, including damianita daisy near the entry and flame acanthus and Spanish lavender by the pool.

# NOW AND ZEN

DALLAS, TEXAS

FRANK WELCH ASSOCIATES

The late Dallas-based architect Frank Welch was a regional modernist. Texas vernacular architecture was a reference point for him—steeply raked metal-seam roofs, tall chimneys, courtyards, porches, arbors, and slatted structural sunshades are manifestations of the inspiration the architect breathed into his designs. The house he designed in Dallas for Bill and Cindy Ward in 2005—and its guest house two years later—reveal the subtle allure of structural understatement when it is paired with total confidence of context.

When the Wards started discussing the project with Welch, they never said a word about how the house should look. "Peaceful, simple, subtle, private, and low maintenance" were the adjectives the Wards used. The resulting 6,500-square-foot, L-shaped two-story stucco-and-glass structure spreads out in front of a lake in the Devonshire neighborhood. It's surrounded by old-growth oak and elm and screened from the street by clusters of Japanese maples. The exterior gives no clue to the experience of walking through the front door and stepping into the light of the open living area. This is, of course, what Welch's work was all about. As a child, he had visited a photographer's studio in his hometown of Sherman, and he was enthralled by the interaction of light with space and materials. Luminescence from above was one of Welch's favorite maneuvers, and in the Ward living area, he used a center skylight to ensure that the room is charged with radiance all day long.

Walls, cabinetry, and the stick ceiling, which covers the three public rooms like an elegant pitched tent, are the beneficiaries of Welch's special illumination. The long, narrow slats of the ceiling add a suggestion of Japanese style to the room, perhaps a nod to Bill Ward's collection of bonsai trees. Interior designer Paul Draper, a student of Japanese design and art, brought in a Japanese mizuya kitchen chest for the living room, but other Zen-like references—such as Draper's use of natural materials and textures for upholstery and floor coverings—are subtle. This kind of transcendence over the mundane was just what the Wards had in mind when they engaged Welch to design their house. "We never discussed design," says Cindy. "We let Frank do whatever he wanted." What Frank Welch wanted was what he always wanted and what he always strove to express: to show light in a way that delights others as much as it did him the very first time he saw it streaming through the photographer's skylight so long ago.

**Preceding spread and left:** Welch designed three white-oak cubes that separate the kitchen and living space and provide space for storage, a powder room, and a pantry. A white-oak slatted-stick ceiling extends over the 1,500-square-foot main living area. Hunks of cypress serve as benches and sculptural punctuation along the window wall. A wood sculpture by Blanco artist Philip John Evett stands in the stairwell. A Holly Hunt pendant light hangs over a Philippine hardwood dining table.

A corner window in the living room displays a resin-coated tablecloth (a family keepsake that once belonged to Cindy Ward's aunt) that Houston artist Joseph Havel has turned into sculpture. Richard Serra prints line the wall to the left of the fireplace. On the mantel, Will Clift's delicate black walnut sculpture *Three Simple Curves* echoes the lines of the Serra prints.

Welch and Draper devised two "reverse" bay windows that flank the front door. These recessed windows include sturdy pedestals to display Bill Ward's bonsai collection. The trees are an architectural detail on either side of the door.

The pool house was one of Welch's last projects. It occupies an adjacent lot the parklike setting. Landscaping by Mary Ellen Cowan of MESA enhances the relationship between the two buildings with dogwood, Koi bamboo, oak leaf hydrangea, Indian hawthorn, and Kurume white azalea.

**Opposite and above:** Draper created a casual setting suitable for guests using the pool. *Song of Summer*—a crape myrtle, dye, and wax piece by Sherry Owens—hangs over the fireplace. **Overleaf:** Screens run the length of the house to add privacy from the street.

GENERAC

# ON
# TOP
# THE
# WORLD

AUSTIN, TEXAS

EDWARD B. FRIERSON ARCHITECT/
JESSICA STEWART LENDVAY

**Preceding spread:** Lueders limestone slabs set in pea gravel mark the approach to the limestone landing and screened breezeway. At the entrance, sculptural shapes such as cactus, a Will Fleming yaupon, and boxwoods are paired with potted ferns and Mexican feather grass. **Opposite:** Complementing the original limestone pavers on the patio is a limestone-clad fireplace with flanking columns.

The dog trot started out humble. In the early days, Texas settlers defaulted to the passageway as they prospered, adding a second building next to a first building and covering the space between with a roof. It was an easy upgrade. Practicality quickly morphed into graciousness: the accommodation was a cool place to enjoy the breeze that always wafted through or to set up a table and dine. These attractions weren't lost on dogs, who found the pathway a convenient shortcut as well as a pleasant place to nap. Their insight is memorialized in the name, but if you called it a breezeway you'd be right, too.

Despite its seeming simplicity, a dog trot can take a very active role in the life of a house. It was the strategy Dallas architect Jessica Stewart Lendvay deployed when she was commissioned to renovate a native-stone and stucco house in the hills west of Austin. "This house had a great sense of place created by architect Edward B. Frierson in the mid-1990s," she says. "It was really well built, a hardy house with thoughtful details on a very dramatic site." With a long driveway that approached the house, the house seemed "other worldly"; thick walls and grand interior spaces gave credence to Lendvay's assessment. She worked with builder David Dalgleish and interior designer Mark Ashby to bring a fresher mein to both the main house and its companion guest house. Although similar in heft, the two buildings are designated as separate by their roofs. The main house is topped with a tile roof; a Galvalume roof caps the guest house.

To take better advantage of the site, the owners asked Lendvay to reorient the interior of the house to the views. "We really opened the house up to the site, which also opened up the interior spaces," she says. She did that by making existing windows bigger, adding bay windows, and enclosing a covered porch (now the dining room) with steel-and-glass windows. Walls and ceilings are plaster, a material with subtle reflective qualities that enlivens the house with luminescence. Because it can be easily shaped with tools, the use of plaster also allowed Lendvay to specify a gracefully curved and ornamented stairwell and to set windows deep into walls. The tactic further informed the feeling that the interiors glow with an inner light. Interior designer Ashby complemented the owners' collection of midcentury Danish furniture with contemporary pieces upholstered in grays.

The house opens at the back to a patio, which overlooks the Austin skyline. As an outdoor destination, it is a powerful invitation to leave the house and enjoy the view. It's buffered from the driveway by a screened-in passageway that connects the area between the main house and the guest house. The connection is a nod to the old-fashioned dog trot, and a special request of the owner who wanted a way for his cats to travel back and forth between the two buildings. "It was one of those things," he says, "that you do for practical reasons, but it ended up being an aesthetic win." The cats triumphed, but the humans also benefited. "There are a lot of good breezes up here," says the owner.

ЭРМИТАЖ

In the living room, wooden doors were replaced with contemporary steel and glass; the wood ceilings are original. Linen curtains soften the space. The furniture is a mix of Danish pieces from the owners' collection—a midcentury coffee table, vintage floor lamps, and Jens Risom lounge chairs—with classics such as the Mies van der Rohe leather daybed.

Floors are wide-planked white-washed white oak, a textural complement to the plaster walls throughout the house. A cylindrical newel at the top of the stair reflects the plasticity of plaster. The family room, now warmed by a Rumford fireplace, occupies the space occupied by the original kitchen.

The panoramic view of the city skyline was revealed once the kitchen windows were enlarged. The steel gridded windows match a nine-pane glass wall that defines the new dining room. The cabinetry is rift-sawn white oak and the counters are crema marfil marble. Formerly a screened porch, the dining room retains the original limestone block walls, a counterpoint to the elegant furnishings.

# POWER OF PLACE

EL PASO, TEXAS

HAZELBAKER RUSH

El Paso is a topographic city, defined as much by formidable geographical extremes as by its location at the intersection of Texas, New Mexico, and Chihuahua, Mexico. The city of nearly 700,000 is in the Chihuahuan Desert just where the Franklin Mountains, the southernmost tip of the Rocky Mountains in the United States, loom large. "It's a city with great character," says Dale Rush, a principal with his wife, Darci Hazelbaker, in the Tucson-based firm Hazelbaker Rush.

When the architects were approached by a couple to design a 5,000-square-foot house 800 feet up the foothills of the Franklin Mountains, the first thing Rush and Hazelbaker did was walk the raw gray-basalt landscape. The site backs up to Franklin Mountains State Park, the largest urban park in the United States, and it has a commanding view of El Paso and Juarez. On a smaller scale, the architects noted the little quartz crystals scattered around the east end of the site, remnants of an abandoned quartz mine up the mountain. "They were beautiful—gemlike and glittering," says Rush.

Rush and Hazelbaker envisioned two shapes that would compose the house for the couple and the two children they planned to have. The sparkling remnants of the mine became the inspiration for the massing of the new house: a modernist white-lime stucco rectangle balanced on and perpendicular to a rectangular building rendered in rubble stone that's characteristic of the city. "The white stucco box was like a piece of quartz," says Rush, "anchored onto rock." The white box houses the bedroom area, "where you dream." Living would take place in the grounded mass underneath. The lower volume closely resembles the surrounding topography; from a distance, the all-white box seems to hover over the severe terrain.

The interior of the house is also inspired by local craft. Darci Hazelbaker designed the black steel hardware, wrapping each pull in leather. The couple made the light fixtures, beds, benches, and the steel-and-wood desks in the office, all by hand. "These projects allowed us to engage with the house," Hazelbaker says. Indeed, this house is about engagement—from the seemingly insignificant, such as the sensation of clasping a door pull—to the all-encompassing, such as how the concrete floors feel underfoot. "The main level of our south-facing house is sided in 40 feet of glass with an 8-foot overhang," says one of the owners. "In winter, the sun can get in and warm the floors. But not in the summer, so the floors stay cool."

The husband is a native Texan, but he had never had the experience of being able to step outside without sweating or fending off mosquitoes. "Here," he says, "it's cool at night and we can leave the doors open." It also seems perfectly natural to the couple's children, now ages 5 and 7, to sit outside and watch helicopters buzz their house. "We are at eye level to them," says their father, "and we can recognize some of the pilots. They'll circle once or twice, and my kids always wave."

Local gray stone—found in rubble walls throughout El Paso—is used for both the retaining walls and the walls of the house. The pattern of the 8-inch-thick pieces of rock is intentionally random, determined by whatever rock the local masons picked up and placed. The resulting texture became the background for the living area of the house. Hazelbaker also did the landscaping, softening the effect of the rock with pink muhly grass and ocotillo. The living room's slot window wraps around the corner to get full exposure to Mount Cristo Rey.

Humble materials such as steel and leather are used throughout the house as a tribute to El Paso's vernacular history as a railroad town and home of Lucchese, the cowboy boot company. All door pulls are handmade in steel wrapped with leather and stitched with waxed thread (a technique used in saddle-making); brass pendant fixtures in the kitchen are custom by Hazelbaker Rush and hang from the ceiling from jute-wrapped cord. Casework in an upstairs hallway is white oak; kitchen cabinetry is walnut.

**Above:** The house is approached via a driveway that ascends the steep slope; entry to the three-story house is through the garage at the first level. Guests arrive on the second level, where the landscape has been terraced, and proceed to the front door. The house sits on two concrete columns that allow for a covered patio and open up a view into Franklin Mountains State Park. **Opposite:** The master bed room opens directly to a gravel terrace.

**Above and opposite:** White oak is used through the master suite for the floors and the bathroom cabinetry. **Overleaf:** An outdoor living area and lap pool extend the length of the living room and kitchen and connect to each other by the same concrete flooring.

# BUILT TO LAST

CASH, TEXAS

BENTLEY TIBBS ARCHITECT

For the convivial Robinson clan—two grandparents, two sons, their wives, and two children each—being together is their idea of a good time. Robby Robinson and his brother, Ryan, are principals in Signal Metal, a steel fabrication business started by their father R. W. in 1973. The elder Robinson grew up on a farm in Oklahoma and bought a ranch in Cash, Texas, in 1982 because he needed some wide-open space that he could just look at.

Nearly every weekend since then the Robinson family has convened there. They eat together, stay up late into the night talking, and fish for bass at dawn in a lake they built. They've made countless improvements to their 400-acre compound in Cash, a farming community fifty miles east of Dallas. Refinements include a 3,500-square-foot two-bedroom house that has grown over the years into a 7,500-square-foot lodge, with a steel bridge to span the lake, a bunkhouse, a swimming pool, and fences.

As both Robby and his wife, Kelly, and Ryan and his wife, Carrie, began having their own children, their ideas about the ranch altered. They began to think of their place as a family legacy. And that's when architect Bentley Tibbs, a protégé of Texas modern regionalist architect Frank Welch, came into the picture. Welch believed that a house design should start with the interior spaces, that the floor plan and the way light enters the spaces and emanates from the materials determines what the exterior ought to be. "The interiority of the house gives it structure and rigor," says Tibbs.

The family turned to Tibbs to develop a way for the group to live both together and separately at the ranch. The general sentiment in the family opposed separate houses, but the notion kept asserting itself. When Tibbs found two sites that overlooked the lake, the architect knew he had the solution. "I designed both houses to be about the basics—sleeping and bathing," Tibbs says. "I didn't want the houses to be so alluring that people would want to stay in them instead of going back to the main house."

The 2,300-square-foot, native stone, cedar, and metal cottages are composed of a series of stone "boxes" and screened porches. Ryan's is made up of five boxes that wind through a grove of oaks, some of which were saplings when the boys transplanted them decades ago. Robby's house consists of three boxes. The design acknowledges the notion of the long sweep of history. If, over the passage of centuries, the wood screened porches fall away from the houses, the open-face stone boxes with their 18-inch-thick walls would remain, like ruins in a small settlement.

This thoughtful architecture defines the narrative of the family's history. And, the legacy continues. Tibbs recently completed another stone cottage, this one for the senior Robinsons, now in their 90s. "They are still going strong," says the architect. There's an explanation for their vitality. "We are always thinking about the next project," says Robby.

**Preceding spread and right:** The living area and kitchen of Robby and Kelly Robinson's cottage focus on what's going on outside. Custom gridded steel windows and doors afford a constant view of the lake beyond, establishing a clear connection between the interior living space and the screened porch. Even the steel cabinets in the kitchen are all glass so that the view predominates.

The master bedroom is predominantly stone, creating a feeling that what is most intimate is also the most permanent part of the house. A window wall with double doors overlooks the lake.

The master bathroom is intentionally spacious and spa-like. The freestanding tub is flanked by clay tiles under a cedar-plank ceiling so that it feels like a separate and special space. A door leads out to a private patio and hot tub.

# MARFA LIGHTS

MARFA, TEXAS

KINNEYMORROW ARCHITECTURE

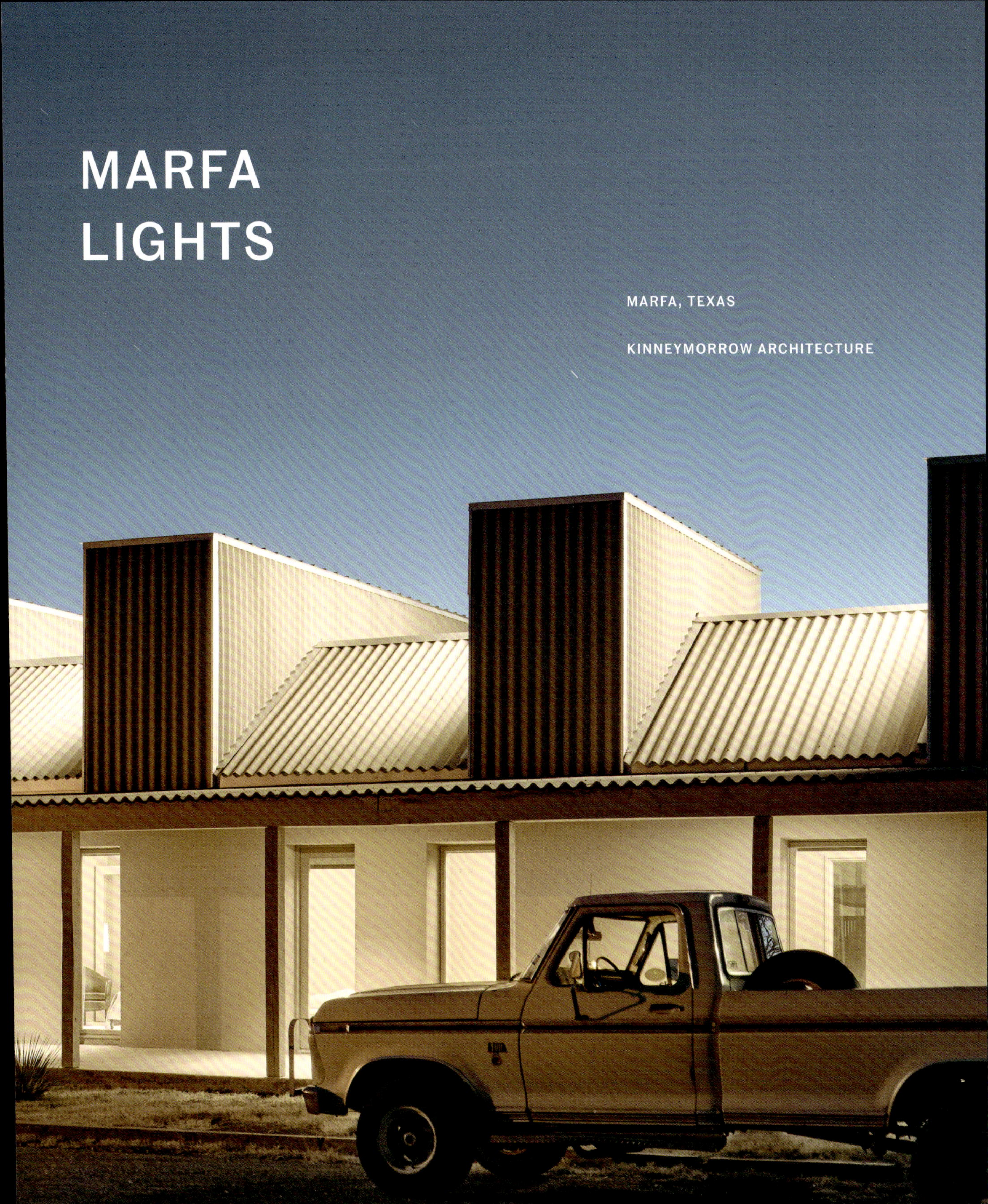

Architect Michael Morrow referenced ranch utility buildings that are ubiquitous in most of Texas as the inspiration for his redesign of the long adobe residence. He added five light boxes on the roof, all sided with Eternit, a corrugated fiber cement material that evokes the corrugated metal roofs that are a staple for agricultural buildings, but in a softer and more textured version.

Marfa has become a destination, if not a refuge, for many city dwellers looking for peace and quiet. They cite the arid high-desert landscape as one reason; the steadfast linearity of its long horizon seems calming. There is magic in Marfa, too, in the vast sky and the light that accompanies this wide-open space—so much of it unencumbered by intervening objects such as trees, buildings, power lines, and other flotsam of modern life. In addition, the sky is an ever-changing scene, and residents enjoy watching storms roll in and stars glitter against the black night sky.

These elements inspired the renovation of a former boarding house near downtown Marfa. The globe-trotting owner, a native of a distant rain-forest region who had moved to Houston, is an art collector. In 2012 he made the nine-hour trek from Houston to Marfa to see the aluminum cubes and other work by Donald Judd as well as Dan Flavin's large-scale pieces in colored fluorescent light on display at the Chinati Foundation. He came to appreciate the easy sociability of the tiny metropolis of 1,747 residents and decided to buy a building. "It was a bit of a beast," the owner recalls about the much-amended long rectangular structure that had been divided into four units to accommodate workers at a nearby tomato farm. At some point in the past, a long porch was added to the back, and it had both stylistically and functionally become an essential part of the house. With the help of Houston architect Michael Morrow and Marfa-based builder Billy Maginot, the decision was made to take the house down to the original adobe, a material that is often used in the area because it can be sourced on site. Its components—mostly earth, water, and straw or dung—are perfectly suited to the climate there, and its earthiness grounded the renovated building in its setting.

That act of grounding, though, presented a problem for both architect and client: the street-level views of nearby dwellings were uninspiring, and the house was dark. Morrow wondered how to embrace the sky, which was what had attracted the peripatetic client to Marfa in the first place. "It dawned on me," he explains," to put lightboxes on the roof so that the house would have views of the sky and also would have light inside." The architect designed five "lanterns," each with glass windows on its south-facing side. The boxes slice east and west, through the roof and into the ceiling, opening up to the interior spaces. "As soon as the sun comes up," says Morrow, "light begins to move through the building, changing from minute to minute as the day progresses." For the owner, a frequent visitor to the James Turrell light composition *Twilight Epiphany Skyspace* at Rice University, the ever-changing display of the materiality of light in his own home was a revelation. "Light has become an active component of the house," he says. At night, too, even without the benefit of illumination, the repetition of rectangular shapes that constitute the house's facade confer on it a primal appeal. "Its profile looks like Stonehenge," the owner observes. And, as befits a place where the importance of art is honored, the owner has discovered that his dwelling developed an identity all its own. "The house," he says, "has turned out to be an *objet d'art.*"

**Above:** The kitchen is intentionally stark with walls reserved for either windows or for art. All appliances are concealed in the quartz-topped island. The stools are by Jeff Covey; pendants are Schoolhouse Electric. **Opposite:** The stools and chairs in the living room are by Garza Marfa; the leather sofa is by Saporetti. Hot Dog Wrapper by Isaac Layman hangs on the wall, which is adobe finished with a layer of Portland cement plaster.

CHINATI

**Preceding spread:** Light from one of the light boxes filters into the living room just above the built-in shelves and the Stuv wood-burning stove. A glimpse of the corrugated fiber cement siding reveals a softness that resembles a curtain. **Opposite:** The plaster-over-adobe walls in the master bedroom serve as the headboard to the custom bed, which is built into custom cabinetry. The blanket over the bed is from Garza Marfa. Floors throughout are poured concrete ground down to reveal the aggregate and then sealed with a matte finish. **Above:** Not all rock is hard in this house where pebble pillows are propped up in a vintage hanging chair, a tongue-in-cheek allusion to the rocky landscape around Marfa.

# BARN DANCE

AUSTIN, TEXAS

BALDRIDGE ARCHITECTS

Passersby strolling down a secluded street on a bluff above Austin's Zilker Park and Barton Springs pool cannot fail to notice the second story of this house floating high above the oak trees that populate the quarter-acre lot. The vertical grain pine barn seems to have settled lightly on its host, a carport and white cement block structure that houses the main living area of the residence.

Designed by Austin architect Burton Baldridge, the three-bedroom dwelling is an exercise in teasing new meaning out of the predictable generalities of modernism. Baldridge's clients—Katie King, senior business development manager for SXSW, and political consultant Matt Parkerson—had asked him to design a modern house that merged indoor and outdoor living. "Everything my firm has done was serious," says Baldridge, who became intrigued by an opportunity to lighten up. "There was supposed to be an element of whimsy in this house."

The playful component pivots on Baldridge's dramatic use of a rural icon, the barn, to announce that he was going to overturn some notions of modernity and challenge the default solution of a house with glass walls that open to the outside. "This is the project where I started to question that strategy," he says.

"Modern is no longer about open and airy—that really doesn't work in Texas. Big expanses of glass don't give you an indoor-outdoor experience." Baldridge finds that strategy claustrophobic, especially at night when those big—and dark—expanses of glass essentially become mirrors reflecting the interior spaces.

Instead, Baldridge tempered access to the landscape by framing transitional spaces so that the outdoors is approached in stages through a hallway or under the protection of a roof like the deck overhang above the patio. Sliding glass doors open, doubling the available space of the living-dining area. An interior courtyard off Parkerson's office invites communion with nature, too, an enclosure that shelters plantings and the viewer from the glare afforded by the intense Texas heat. A deck at the front of the house projects into a shaded canopy of trees; in back a deck off the master bedroom is embraced on both sides and at the top by walls and a pitched ceiling. The screened porch, just off the living room and sharing its fireplace, offers another opportunity to be outside. Ever-present, and the centerpiece around which the house is built, is the inviting pool. "This is where we spend most of our time," says King. "The house has made us love the Texas heat."

The upper volume of this house is an extruded gable that extends out in front to form the car port and over the back, framing the outdoor spaces and providing shade over the patio.

Modern Art
Modern Art
100 CONTEMPORARY HOUSES
100
CONTEMPORARY HOUSES

The ground floor is a seamless loop of public spaces, with a series of changes in level both inside and out that conform to the sloping grade of the lot. The multiple levels inside the house define functionality of space in the open plan.

**Opposite:** The double-sided fireplace, executed in custom-cut charcoal Lueders limestone, helps to unite the screened porch with the living room.
**Above:** The interlocking forms and dramatic cantilever are welcoming from the street.

# ROCKING RANCH

WEATHERFORD, TEXAS

LAKE|FLATO ARCHITECTS

For the architects at Lake|Flato, the goal is always to find ways to encourage people to be outside. In the case of Rocking X Ranch, though, that agenda was already firmly in place. "We are outside all the time here," says Lou Cagle, the owner of the 8,000-acre ranch. The ranch is atop the North Texas rolling plains between Weatherford and Granbury, with the Brazos River running right next to it. Cagle approached Lake|Flato to assist her in figuring out how she, her husband, Mike, their three sons, and her mother—plus an array of sisters, cousins, nieces, and nephews—could enjoy the ranch together and apart.

"We wanted to be simple and direct," says project architect Brian Comeaux, "and to use the existing five-bedroom ranch house as the anchor in a compound." Cagle liked that idea because it meant that some could stay up late in the big game room she was envisioning and others could happily sleep through the night in the new casitas that were the key to the plan.

The formal cues for the new buildings sprang from the ranch's own vernacular—farm structures, sheds, and out buildings already located throughout the property. The game room lives up to Cagle's vision, and probably goes well beyond it. The building encourages more than games, with a pool table, shuffleboard table, a round table for dining or playing board games, and the kitchen with bar seating. Cagle did her own decorating, providing plenty of comfortable chairs and sofas for lounging around a coffee table or in front of the fire. The two-bedroom, two-bath casitas are connected to the rock, steel, and glass game room by a network of arbor-covered pathways that also leads to a service building housing a motor court, laundry, mud room, and storage. The system of pathways assures at least five degrees of separation between the buildings. It also guarantees that family and guests interact with the weather, the views, and the topography (and maybe even an occasional rattlesnake that's cooling off between the dry-stack rocks in the wall bordering the pathway).

**Above and overleaf:** Steel-and-cedar arbor-covered walkways connect all the buildings and relate to a grove of oaks in the courtyard at the side of the house. Horizontal slats screen the view of cars so as not to distract from the panoramic view from the edge of the bluff beyond. Gravel paths were built wide enough to make it easy to spot rattlesnakes.

The game room is open to the west, but the fireplace blocks the sun and a four-foot overhang protects the southern exposure. Floors are scored concrete and always cool underfoot in the summer. Overhead in the living area and porch, the ceiling is Douglas fir planks with raw steel supporting beams.

# MODEL FORD

SAN ANTONIO, TEXAS

O'NEIL FORD / TOBIN SMITH ARCHITECT

"This is a house with a lot of history," says San Antonio architect Tobin Smith. And, it's not afraid to show it. The pink brick and Saltillo tile residence is a heartening example of a house designed by O'Neil Ford that still is essentially in original condition. That's remarkable enough, considering the American penchant for demolishing the old, which has sadly included some Ford-designed houses. But it's also remarkable because the house—built in 1958—has remained in good condition. It has been served well by its two owners, but it also survives because of Ford's insistence on using natural materials—"old-age insurance for buildings," he called them.

The public and private spaces are separate volumes, connected by a glass core. The house sits near the edge of a 60-foot bluff and has a view to the horizon, a rare thing in San Antonio. Ford aligned the sightlines of the house with Basse Road far below, so the house is invigorated by a relationship with the busy thoroughfare in the distance. It's both urban and rural, and when the new owners approached Tobin Smith to help them refresh the property, it was its spectacular setting that everyone agreed needed attention. "We never had a discussion about updating the kitchen, for instance," says the owner. "But the outside had had nothing done to it, and the impetus was a crack in the retaining wall. We never knew what rain or breeze would be the one to take it down."

Changes that were deeply pragmatic, such as redefining the front parking area and building a new retaining wall to stabilize the failing terrace, blossomed into aesthetic results. Smith devised ways to extend the lines of the house into the grounds and to animate the interior and exterior with courtyards and perimeter spaces that had been implied in the original footprint of the house. A new central patio, referred to as "the runway terrace," directs the viewer to look out from the main entry through the glass core to a new negative-edge pool that merges with the horizon and accentuates the strong central axis of the house. The cliff at the end of the site has now been integrated into the daily experience of the house, emphatically joining the house to the activity of the major city street in the distance.

"When Tobin arrived," says the owner, "it changed the way we lived in this house." Now that the grounds are assimilated into the living space, the house thrives on a grand scale—at 20,674 square feet, this flawlessly scaled building extends its boundaries. "Every day we are outside, rain or shine, heat or cold," says the owner. The house has become more than it ever was. Architect O'Neil Ford built that possibility into everything he designed. It's the lesson the visionary urged on anyone who would listen, that architecture is the knowledge of the possibilities of materials. In this house, Ford ensured that the possibilities were endless.

**Preceding spread:** The teak front doors, carved by O'Neil Ford's brother Lynn, are original to the house. **Opposite:** An abstract painting by Kathy Green hangs on an orange wall in the entry. **Above:** An abstract painting by Lewis Tarver and a leather, felt, and paper collage by Constance Lowe hang on the living room wall.

TIM FLACH DOGS

Pink Mexican brick—a favorite building material of Ford's—is used on both the facade and interior walls. The soaring Douglas fir ceilings in the living room overarch original gridded windows that, in some rooms, are floor-to-ceiling. A sculpture by Laddie John Dill hangs over the fireplace in the living room.

Douglas fir cabinetry and doors are original to the kitchen, which the owners have kept intact. Punched copper-and-lead cabinetry inserts are by Judith Maxwell (widow of long-time Ford collaborator architect Isaac Maxwell) and Gregorio Rebollar, Maxwell's chief fabricator. Midcentury chairs complement the rustic farm table.

Bringing Nature Home

Ford used the same gridded motif for sliding doors in the sitting room that he employed throughout the house. A vintage landscape hangs above a Milo Baughman green velvet sofa; the chairs are Scandinavian, and the table base is by Vladimir Kagan. The pink brick wall is the backdrop for a lime-green tufted and upholstered headboard in a daughter's bedroom.

The renovation included the gardens, where Smith redefined the front parking area, built a new retaining wall to stabilize the terrace, and extended the lines of the house into the grounds to stitch interior and exterior spaces together. Smith used Saltillo tile—a preferred Ford building material—for exterior patios; concrete and river stones define outdoor spaces. **Overleaf:** The brass numerals on the entry wall are original, created by San Antonio metalsmith Denise Kocurek when she was Lynn Ford's fabrication assistant.

ONE ROCK RIDGE

## CREDITS

### THINGS SEEN AND UNSEEN

Architect: Steve Raike, Lake|Flato
Interior Design: Poët Interiors
Landscape Design: Ten Eyck Landscape Architects

### UPLIFTED

Architect: Michael Hsu Office of Architecture
Interior Design: Laura Roberts Design
Landscape Design: MADRONE

### URBAN OUTLOOK

Architect: Max Levy Architect
Interior Design: Sharon Odum Architect
Landscape Design: Susie Thompson,
Thompson Landscape Architects

### CLIFFHANGER

Original architect: Jonathan Bowman;
Architecture and Interior Design: Pollen Architecture & Design
Landscape Design: Studio Balcones and Michael Young,
Pollen Architecture & Design

### CULTURED CLUB

Original Architect: O'Neil Ford
Architecture and Interior Design: Bodron+Fruit
Landscape Design: MESA

### COOL, CALM, AND COLLECTED

Architecture and Interior Design: Marcus Mohon Interiors.

### SPEAK TO ME

Architect: Hugh Jefferson Randolph Architects
Interior Design and Landscape Design: Gina O'Hara

### SITE SPECIFIC

Original Architect: Bud Oglesby
Architects: Lawrence W. Speck and Jason Smith
Interior Design: Emily Summers Design Associates
Landscape Design: MESA

### REMEMBRANCE OF THINGS PAST

Architect: Paul Lamb Architects
Interior Design: Susan Ferrier, McAlpine, Booth & Ferrier
Landscape Design: D-Crain Design and Construction

**VIEWFINDER**

Architect: Lemmo Architecture and Design

**ROCK SOLID**

Architect: Rebecca B. Comeaux, Lake|Flato

Interior Design: Owner

Landscape Design: Ten Eyck Landscape Architects

**NOW AND ZEN**

Architect: Frank Welch Associates

Interior Design: Paul Draper

Landscape Design: MESA

**ON TOP OF THE WORLD**

Original Architect: Edward B. Frierson

Architect: Jessica Stewart Lendvay Architects

Interior Design: Michele Lorenz, Mark Ashby Design

Landscape Design: David Wilson Garden Design

**POWER OF PLACE**

Architecture, Interior Design, and Landscape Design: Hazelbaker Rush

**BUILT TO LAST**

Architect: Bentley Tibbs Architect

Interior Design: Kelly Robinson

Landscape Design: Hocker Design Group

**MARFA LIGHTS**

Architecture and Interior Design: kinneymorrow architecture

**BARN DANCE**

Architecture and Landscape Design: Baldridge Architects

**ROCKING RANCH**

Architect: Brian Comeaux, Lake|Flato

**MODEL FORD**

Original Architect: O'Neil Ford

Architecture and Landscape Design: Tobin Smith Architect

## ACKNOWLEDGMENTS

In conceiving this book, Casey Dunn and I had something very specific in mind: to show how modernism took its own shape and went its own way in Texas. The people whose houses we show in these pages understand that their homes are special, either because they specifically asked for them to be or because they recognized the uniqueness in an older home they bought and renovated.

It is these owners we thank, for seeing the Texan-ness in their residences, for striving to preserve those sui generis traits, and especially for wanting others to see and know why a very specific architectural interpretation was relevant when it started and is even more relevant today.

*Texas Made/Texas Modern* wouldn't have been possible without the help of Elizabeth Alford and Michael Young, Janet and Wilson Allen, Lou and Mike Cagle, Toby and Emma Calvert, David and Kathy Clem, Katie King and Matt Parkerson, Gina and Bill O'Hara, Deborah Orill and Blair Sanders, Robby and Kelly Robinson, Bill and Cindy Ward, and last, but not least, the owners who wish to remain anonymous.

Thanks especially to photographic assistant Allen Corralejo and to our families and extended family: Ruth Smith, Tommy, Beverly, and Avery Dunn, Sarah Dunn, and Jenn Dunn. Special thanks to our editor Elizabeth White, whose steady guidance and wholehearted support gave us the book we dreamed of having. Special thanks, too, to designer Cody Haltom for remaining with us and keeping our team intact. Cody's elegant design is a reminder that books aren't just meant to be read but to be looked at, touched, and relished.

For Casey W.

Monacelli
A Phaidon Company
111 Broadway
New York, NY 10006

Phaidon Press Limited
2 Cooperage Yard
London E15 2QR

Phaidon SARL
55, rue Traversière
75012 Paris

phaidon.com/monacelli


First published in the United States by The Monacelli Press.

Library of Congress Control Number: 2018945393
ISBN: 978-1-58093-5-081

Printed in China
Designed by Cody Haltom